PAPER LANTERNS, PAPER CRANES

a play by

Brian Kral

copyright 1984
unpublished manuscript by the author

copyright 2002
Anchorage Press Plays, Inc
Louisville KY USA
ISBN 0-87602-404-5

ii

Without the generosity
of Karen McKenney—
first as an actress
and later as a producer—
this script would not have reached the stage
or the printed page.
All gratitude
and sincere thanks

"Not only is it impossible to forecast when and what kind of disease will appear...but it may be said that no one who has been exposed to the atomic bomb will ever be relieved from its consequences."

The Committee for the Compilation of Materials on Damages Caused by the Atomic Bombs

"This is our cry, this is our prayer; peace in the world."

Inscription on the Children's Monument in Hiroshima

*   *   *

PAPER LANTERNS, PAPER CRANES was first performed by the Rainbow Company Children's Theatre on October 5, 1984, in Las Vegas, Nevada. It was directed by Mary Hall Surface*, with the following cast:

KYUSHU	Pat Ball
DR. TAKAMURA	Ken Kucan
DR. FRIZZEL	Karen McKenney
THE ATTENDANT	Mark S. Nicholl
SADAKO	Kristy-Lynn Skupa
SADAKO's FATHER	Thomas R. Dyer
COCKROACH WOMAN	Sydney Minckler
LILLY	Dabney Evans
SCHOOL CHILDREN	
/CHORUS:	David Cherry
	Aviva Morger,
	Dabney Evans,
	Ronna Wiseman,
	David Adler

Costume Designs were by Dale Segal; Set Design and Technical Direction were by Thomas Dyer, with Lighting Design by Stephen Mathews. The production's Stage Manager was Ken Evans.

* Ms. Surface was in residence with the Rainbow Company through an artist exchange with the California Theatre Center.

*   *   *

PAPER LANTERNS, PAPER CRANES was subsequently a finalist for the IUPUI Children's Theatre Playwriting Competition, and was given a staged reading at the University Theatre, Indiana University-Purdue University at Indianapolis.

The Setting:

The action takes place in a hospital in Hiroshima during the '50s, but it can be performed against the non-realistic background of an over-sized folding, Japanese-style fan. The hospital can be created through the use of selected furnishings: hospital beds and tables, and moveable masking partitions.

The setting should be both mysterious and frightening, but remain flexible enough to accommodate each of Kyushu's shifts in thought and feeling, as the surrounding action often is designed to mirror her personal confusion.

Characters:

KYUSHU, a teenage girl
SADAKO, a twelve-year-old girl
DR. TAKAMURA, a Japanese physician (male, 35-55 yrs. old)
DR. FRIZZEL, an American researcher (female, 30-45)
THE ATTENDENT (male, adult)
THE NURSE (female, adult)
SADAKO's FATHER (30-45)
THE COCKROACH WOMAN (20-35)
TWO STRETCHER -BEARERS (male, adult)
JAPANESE SCHOOLCHILDREN: First Girl
                                  Older Boy
                                  Smaller Boy
                                  Little Girl
LILLY, Dr. Frizzel's daughter (8-10 yrs. old)
JAPANESE WOMAN, the small boy's mother (20-30)

Doubling can be accomplished in the following roles: Stretcher-bearers can be played by Sadako's Father and the Older Boy; Lilly, the Schoolchildren, the Nurse and the Japanese Woman should all be included in the opening procession; the Japanese Boy who is admitted to the hospital late in the play can be one of Sadako's visiting classmates from the earlier scene.

SYNOPSIS OF SCENES

Procession: August 6, 1945: A group of Japanese Schoolchildren witness the explosion of the atomic bomb in Hiroshima

Scene One: Mid 50's: A teenage street-child named Kyushu is admitted into a hospital. She is interrogated by doctors about her health and failing eyesight, but she refuses to cooperate with them. She's haunted by a figure from the Hiroshima blast, called the Cockroach Woman. Shouting in her sleep, Kyushu wakes and meets another patient, a twelve year-old named Sadako.

Scene Two: Sadako is visited by her father and children from her school. Kyushu is told by the doctors that she will undergo more tests. Sadako and Kyushu discuss A-bomb sickness, and Sadako shows her an origami paper crane she's folded.

Scene Three: Kyushu catches the hospital Attendant stealing from Sadako at night while the younger girl is asleep. He tells Kyushu that everything's fair and everyone's looking out for themselves. In quick succession, Kyushu is questioned by the Physician, Dr. Takamura, and an American psychologist, Dr. Frizzel, until Kyushu finally admits that she was in Hiroshima during the A-bomb blast. Sadako tries cheering her up by teaching her to fold a paper crane.

Scene Four: Kyushu's spirits improve, but Sadako appears to be getting worse. A Japanes Woman visits Sadako with one of the Schoolchildren (the Small Boy.) He reminds Kyushu that she is an A-bomb victim, and then the Cockroach Woman returns to haunt her again. The Attendant warns Kyushu that Sadako won't live much longer.

Scene Five: Kyushu gives up, feeling that recovery is hopeless, and ignores the recommendations of both doctors. She catches the Attendant removing Sadako's things, and again accuses him of stealing. Dr. Frizzel tells Kyushu that Sadako has died. Kyushu agrees to surgery.

Scene Six: Dr. Takamura performs the surgery on Kyushu's eyes. While she recuperates, she is visited one more time by the Cockroach Woman, but this time Kyushu speaks to her. The girl brings peace to the woman's ghost by giving her water to drink. When Kyushu's bandages are removed, her eyesight is clearer. She is introduced to Lilly, Dr. Frizzel's daughter. Kyushu shows the young American girl how to fold an origami crane.

Approximate running time: 1 hr. 40 minutes, with intermission.

PAPER LANTERNS, PAPER CRANES

PROCESSION

An oversized Japanese fan stands open, dominating the performance area.

An orange glow rises slowly, suggesting the first light of sunrise. A procession of JAPANESE SCHOOLCHILDREN enters, singing a traditional song. A small child in the front carries a long bamboo pole, from which is suspended a colorful paper lantern.

They stop in arbitrary arrangement, in front of the large fan, continuing their singing. But as the song continues, the drone of an airplane and the dull static of an airplane's radio transmitter are slowly noticed, growing in volume.

VOICE OF AMERICAN PILOT (over)

Fair weather. Ready for air raid. Proceed to primary target.

(The drone of the airplane's engines catches the attention of the children. They stop their song, staring up at the sound of the plane. Long pause, as the sound mesmerizes those who hear it. A bright white light flashes suddenly. The children shield their eyes against the light, then react to the wave of heat that strikes them—subtly, as they would to an uncomfortably hot gust of wind. The paper lantern ignites unexpectedly, burning quickly away, and the children slowly sink to the ground. The daylight is smudged by an ominous dark cloud.)

JAPANESE BROADCAST (over)

Japanese Imperial Headquarters today verified that yesterday morning at 8:16 Hiroshima was attacked by B-29s....Details are not yet confirmed, but it appears the planes dropped a new type of bomb....Damages will continue to be investigated.

(As broadcast ends, the children rise to slowly fold the large fan and remove it.)

1

SCENE ONE

In the area previously concealed by the fan is a hospital bed. Lying in the bed is KYUSHU, a Japanese teenager. A simple white sheet covers her as she sleeps.

The children from the procession carry the fan to the rear of the stage. Two children may remain standing by it; the others sit in a semi-circle on the floor, defining the upstage limits of the acting space. They will occasionally accent the events in the hospital with Oriental wind and percussion instruments—but, more importantly, act as witnesses to all the actions in the hospital.

Kyushu twists uncomfortably on the bed, struggling with the sheet and eventually throwing it off of her.

KYUSHU

It's so hot. Could I have a drink of water? Toshi?

(A percussive accent from the children. Kyushu swings her legs down off the bed with difficulty.)

Hell. Where am I?

(A NURSE enters, and pulls aside a white masking panel. Behind it is revealed DR. TAKAMURA, a middle-aged physician in hospital dress, standing behind a table.)

TAKAMURA

You were asleep. You needed rest.

KYUSHU (to herself)

I need some water.

(On the opposite side, a matching panel is also pulled out, revealing DR. FRIZZEL, an American researcher. She has a clip-board. Kyushu tries to stand.)

2

TAKAMURA

You shouldn't try to walk.

KYUSHU

Why not?

TAKAMURA

You're too weak.

KYUSHU (stepping away from the bed)

That's a lot of—

(Without the bed's support, she collapses to the floor. The American doctor writes something on her clipboard. Takamura steps forward, but before he can reach Kyushu, a slovenly dressed ATTENDANT hurries over, to help her back into bed.)

ATTENDANT (whispering)

Little fool! Listen to the doctors.

(He retreats into the shadowy recesses surrounding the bed.)

KYUSHU

Is this a hospital? How'd I get here?

TAKAMURA

Soldiers brought you.

KYUSHU

Am I sick?

TAKAMURA (speaking with precision)

Maybe. Maybe only tired.

KYUSHU

And maybe sick and tired, hah?

(She laughs, looking at the large room.)

FRIZZEL (to Takamura)

She speaks English well.

3

                              TAKAMURA
Most of them do. It's a byproduct of your Occupation.

                              KYUSHU (indignantly)
"Them?"
                              (She shrugs it off.)
Where's Toshi?

                              FRIZZEL
Your friend left. I think he was afraid of the American soldiers.

                              KYUSHU
He was afraid of the <u>police</u>. Americans don't bother him.

                              FRIZZEL (writing something on clip
                              board)
What about you?

                              KYUSHU
You one?

                              FRIZZEL
That's right.

                              KYUSHU
"Tokio kid say. Amerikans A-okay'"

                              TAKAMURA (stepping to the bed)
I'm Doctor Takamura, head physician here. This is Dr Leigh Frizzel, with the
Atomic Bomb Casualty Council's research group.

                              KYUSHU
The what?

                              TAKAMURA (low, to Kyushu)
Get used to her; you'll be seeing plenty of each other.
                              (Nurse rolls over a table of intruments.
                              Takamura begins to examine Kyushu.
                              The sound accompaniment intensifies.)

                              FRIZZEL (stepping to opposite side
                              of bed)
I'll be asking you things, about your past.
                              (Takamura takes Kyushu's pulse-rate.)

                              4

KYUSHU (to Frizzel)

I haven't got any.

TAKAMURA

Open your mouth please.

FRIZZEL

Are you from Tokyo?

KYUSHU (as Takamura probes her gums)

Nah. Hiroshima. All my life.

(Frizzel writes something on clipboard. Kyushu pulls free of Takamura.)

Hey, why're you writing that down?

TAKAMURA

We're writing everything down. Turn your head.

(He exams Kyushu's ears with a light.)

KYUSHU

I don't like it....The A-bomb was over ten years ago. It doesn't have anything to do with me.

TAKAMURA (shining a light in her eyes)

Eyes wide.

KYUSHU

And you, writing it all down—makes me feel like I'm on trial.

FRIZZEL (retreating into the shadows)

It shouldn't. Relax.

(The sounds strike a sudden resolution. Takamura steps back, thinking. Then he moves to the side, to dictate some notes to the Nurse, who also has a clipboard.)

KYUSHU

What is it? What's the matter?

TAKAMURA (to the Nurse)

There's some indication...of ocular lesions...thermal scarring on both eyelids.

5

TAKAMURA (To Kyushu:)
Have you noticed any visual disorders, any distortions?

KYUSHU
What...?—I don't know what you mean?

FRIZZEL
Any changes in the way you see?

KYUSHU
Nah. I see you both fine. Can you cure that?

TAKAMURA
How many fingers am I holding up?

KYUSHU
Why?

(Takamura waits, his patience thin.)
Three!...Sixteen!...Fifty-five...

(The Nurse notes this on her clipboard.

I'm sorry, Sensai. Sometimes I get my questions confused. "What year is it?" "How old are you?" "What number of fingers do you see?" So many questions, from you, the police, the soldiers. They all...blend...together.
(Kyushu drops back on the bed, re-
solved to remain stubbornly silent.)

TAKAMURA
Well, we're going to ask you a lot of questions, and for your sake, I hope you'll be prepared to answer them, and answer them honestly. Otherwise, we won't do you any good.
(He writes on the nurse's clipboard.)
We're not going to perform any major tests for now. We want to give you a day or two with food, and see if your strength comes back.

KYUSHU (to herself)
If I get my strength back, you won't be doing any tests.

TAKAMURA
What did you say?

(Kyushu doesn't respond.)
You're here for a reason. Think about that. And if you don't want to cooperate, I'll give my time to someone who wishes to be helped.

(Dr. Takamura leaves, followed by the
Nurse.)

KYUSHU (calling after him)
What "good" do you think you can do me?

FRIZZEL (answering the question
calmly)
We don't know yet. We don't know what's wrong with you.

KYUSHU
You don't know a hell of a lot, do you?

FRIZZEL
Not yet. But, as Dr. Takamura said, if you'd cooperate, we'd know a lot
more, and maybe be able to help you.
(Slight pause.)
Why doesn't Toshi like the police?

KYUSHU
Because every time someone gets robbed, we get questioned. They're not
very nice about it, either. One time they beat him up. So don't expect to
see him around here....
(She looks around, finally studying her
surroundings.)
Why'd they bring me to a hospital?

FRIZZEL (writing on the clipboard)
To make you better. You collapsed on the street. Soldiers helped you here.

KYUSHU
Yeah? Big help.
(Tapping the back of her clipboard.)
And what's all that? What's it for?

FRIZZEL
To make others better—who might have been affected by the fallout.

KYUSHU (suddenly angry)
Well, I'm not interested in them. And you thought about them a little too
late! Best thing you could do for all of us—starting with me—is to leave us
all alone.

7

                        FRIZZEL
Is that what you want?

                        KYUSHU
I told you before: I want something to drink!...How about it, Amerika-san?
Could you get me a tall glass of water?
                                (Frizzel takes a pitcher of water and a
                                glass from a bedside table, pours it
                                for Kyushu. She drinks it quickly. A
                                twelve-year-old Japanese girl named
                                SADAKO is led in by her FATHER and
                                Dr. Takamura. The Attendant rushes
                                in with a sheet and a pillow, quickly
                                making up an unmade bed. He stays
                                on the side as Sadako hops up onto
                                the bed. Kyushu watches this.)

                        KYUSHU (turning back to the
                        American)
You talk to a lot of A-bomb victims?

                        FRIZZEL
Quite a few.

                        KYUSHU
How'd you get here?

                        FRIZZEL
My husband's in the military. He came here with our Occupation forces,
and wrote me what was happening. And then I applied for a research posi-
tion. I'm a scientist, Kyushu. Psychology.

                        KYUSHU
You say that like I'm supposed to know something about it.

                        FRIZZEL (amused)
I think you know a lot more about human psychology than you realize.

                        KYUSHU
Hah? Maybe....

                        TAKAMURA (to Sadako)
We don't want to frighten you. So we won't do any tests today. You see?
Hospitals aren't really so bad.

                                8

KYUSHU (low, to Dr. Frizzel)

Does she have A-bomb disease?

FRIZZEL (looking across at the little girl)

I don't know her case. But not necessarily.

(Kyushu turns away, not watching.)

KYUSHU

Sure.

TAKAMURA (continuing to Sadako)

We want you to rest, and be comfortable.

(He pats her hand, and moves to the rear of the room. Frizzel continues to watch Sadako with her father, but Kyushu still avoids looking at them.)

FATHER

Everything O-K?

(Sadako nods. Her father remains briefly, then joins Takamura. They exit, talking.)

FRIZZEL (to Kyushu)

We'll talk again tomorrow, Kyushu.

(She exits in a different direction than Takamura. The hospital has fallen silent, marking a movement to late afternoon. Sadako unpacks a few things she brought from home, arranging them on her bed; Kyushu tosses and turns, struggling to relax in this unnatural environment. The Attendant enters, notes the absence of doctors, and rushes to Kyushu's bed.)

ATTENDANT (with mock reverence)

"Sensai!" "Wise guy." *Little fool*...You should <u>listen</u> to them. Although there's nothing they can do for you either.

(He takes Kyushu's glass, dumps the remaining water into a bucket he's carrying.)

But you don't listen to anyone, do you? You know everything.

9

KYUSHU

What is there to know?

ATTENDANT

How long you'll live.
(Smiling.)
That's all there is to know for anyone,...Sensai.
(Pause.)
You want some American cigarettes, or movie magazines? For cash I can get you anything you like.

KYUSHU

I'm supposed to be resting.

ATTENDANT (solicitously)

Yes, you need rest, so you can feel healthier.
(He smiles, then adds confidentially.)
That little girl, she has genbakusho too.

KYUSHU

That's not what the doctor said.

ATTENDANT

Who you going to believe?—them or me?
(Slight pause.)
Too bad, eh, a little girl like that, with the A-bomb sickness? She might not even know it. And if she does, she wouldn't tell you. First, you know, they deny it—"Hitei shiyo!"—and pretend they don't have it. But finally, they all become resigned to it: "O, akirame..."

KYUSHU (turning away)

I don't have anything to do with that.
(He looks at her, weighing his strategy.)

ATTENDANT (smiling)

No. 'Course not.
(He begins tucking in the corners of her sheets, as if she weren't in the bed.)
These A-bomb victims—these "hibakusha," they call themselves—they come here all the time. You'd think they'd just stay home, so no one could tell them, "Yes, you have the A-bomb disease, you too will die soon."
(Continuing his work, quickly, adroitly.)

10

ATTENDANT (continued)

You'd think they'd stay hidden in their houses, where they don't have to hear the truth, and where no one would see them. Until the poison eats through their bodies. I say let them stay there!

> (He has smoothed the sheets, and now begins scrubbing the floor with a large sponge from his bucket.)

But not these hibakusha. They're proud, they expect privileges! "We want money for standing under the bomb! We want recognition for suffering!"

KYUSHU

Maybe they want to make sure there are no more bombs.

ATTENDANT (suddenly angry)

Who listens to them? Haven't the Americans gone on and on, continuing their bombings? Those simple fishermen, in the Bikini Islands—dead from radiation sickness—what good did complaints of the hibakusha do them? No, the Americans are a great people—you must be great to build such a weapon. So why should they listen to the cries and whimpers of the A-bomb victims? The only ones who have to hear them are us!

> (He scrubs at the floor furiously.)

I don't pity the hibakusha, our "afflicted ones." Most people look at them and sigh, "Kawaiso..."[How pitiful.]* But I say "Baka!" [Stupid!] I offer them no special coddling here, it's not my fault the bomb fell on Hiroshima. And if the Americans dropped a bomb on me tomorrow, I would throw up my hands and smile at that splendid mushroom cloud in the sky. "Shogonai," I'd say: "It can't be helped."

> (Silence. Sadako's Father returns to her bedside, and silently says goodbye to his daughter. He exits. Attendant watches, then resumes his scrubbing and orating.)

It is a damn pity, though, to have a daughter like that who's going to die. All because of the A-bomb. I'd hate to be father to a child who—

KYUSHU (turning on him)

Shut up! Is that all you can talk about?

ATTENDANT

What's the matter, Sensai? Afraid of a little death?

KYUSHU

No...

ATTENDANT (smiling)
You're afraid of something. I can smell it.

KYUSHU
I just don't want to talk about...something you know nothing about.

ATTENDANT
I know plenty about it. I see it all the time.
(He tosses his sponge into the bucket.)

KYUSHU
Do you have to talk about it?

ATTENDANT (picking up his bucket)
No. I don't have to talk about anything.

KYUSHU
You don't even know if she's sick! You're not a doctor!

ATTENDANT (starting out)
Then don't believe me!—See for yourself.

KYUSHU (low, as he is leaving)
How do you know she's going to die?

ATTENDANT (stopping abruptly)
How do I know?...Because they all do.
(He exits, carrying off the bucket. Pause. Sadako has fallen asleep. Kyushu again struggles with her sheets uncomfortably, finally throwing them off. With a great effort, she succeeds in sitting up, only to fall back once more, exhausted.

From a dark corner of the room appears the figure of the COCKROACH WOMAN. Her skin and dress are burnt, and covered in dark ash and dirt, giving her an overall effect of having a dull, hard coating. Her facial features are almost indiscernible, except for large red-rimmed eyes.)

COCKROACH WOMAN

Mizu. Dozo. Mizu-wo kudasai. *[Water. Please. Give me water.]

> (Kyushu turns away. The figure steps towards her.)

Mizu...Mizu...Mizu-wo sukoshi kudasai. [Water...Water...Give me some water.] (Kyushu curls up and covers her head,attempting to shut out all memory of the Cockroach woman. The figure holds out her hands.)

Dozo. Anata-wa...mizu-wo...motte-imasuka? [Please. Do you have...water?]

KYUSHU

Please! Go away!

> (The figure remains frozen, her hands outstretched. Sadako sits up, but cannot see the Cockroach woman. Whispered:)

Can't you...leave me in peace.

SADAKO

Who are you talking to?

> (Kyushu spins around to see the girl, then back to face the figure, which is now slowly shambling out.)

You shouted. It woke me....Were you having a dream?...

KYUSHU (staring at the retreating figure)

Yes. I am.

SADAKO

What was it?

KYUSHU (as the figure disappears)

Nothing.

> (Kyushu lies down, pulling up the sheet.)

Leave me alone.

> (Sadako watches the older girl, who is awake but avoids Sadako's glance.)

---

*Dialogue in brackets [ ] is translated for the actor's use, and is not to be spoken

SCENE TWO

The schoolchildren enter, singing a
traditional Japanese folk-song, light
and uplifting. They gather around
Sadako's bed, followed by her Father,
and as the song concludes, he leads
the applause. Takamura has entered,
and is checking Kyushu's eyes.

FATHER

And after they sang, they had the graduation. And the principal noted how
sad they all were...that you couldn't be there.

FIRST GIRL

We missed you!

SADAKO

I wish I could've been there.

OLDER BOY

But, since your father refused to let you out of the hospital,..
                              (There is laughter at this, and Sadako
                              takes her father's hand.)
...we decided to bring your graduation certificate...
                              (He holds it up for her to see.)
...and have a celebration here.

SADAKO (taking the certificate)

Thank you, Hiroshi.

FIRST GIRL

And we brought presents! Candies, and books, and—

OLDER BOY

Quiet, Hatsuko! Let her see them for herself.
                              (As Sadako unwraps her gifts, a large
                              apparatus is wheeled in to test
                              Kyushu's eyesight, completely cover-
                              ing her face.)

SADAKO

Ooo. Look at this.

(Kyushu tries to turn, in order to see.)

TAKAMURA (to Kyushu)

Stay put, please.

(Kyushu turns back to face the machine.)

SADAKO (holding up a plastic bag)

Rice candies!

SMALLER BOY (whispering)

Can you have them in the hospital?

FATHER (also whispering)

We just won't tell the doctors.

(There is more laughter from the group.)

SADAKO

But there's so many. You'll have to help me eat them.

(She holds out the bag, and the boy digs in happily.)

FIRST GIRL (slapping his hand)

Just one, Matsuo.

(The boy smiles as he pops the rice candy into his mouth.)

OLDER BOY

There's a diary, too. To write down the horrors they inflict on you here.

KYUSHU (from behind machine)

I can write that chapter.

TAKAMURA (checking results)

Keep quiet, Kyushu.

FATHER (ushering a small girl forward)

And little Genko-chan has something special for you, too, Sadako.

LITTLE GIRL (holding out a package)

My brother Iri and I bought it, with money mother gave us for the festival.

(Sadako unwraps it.)

They're origami papers. Your father says you folded a whole packet already.

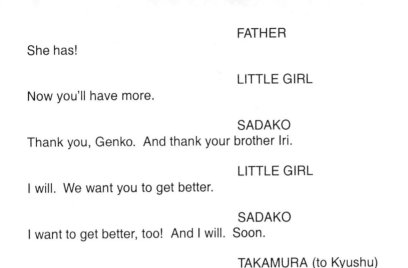

FATHER

She has!

LITTLE GIRL

Now you'll have more.

SADAKO

Thank you, Genko. And thank your brother Iri.

LITTLE GIRL

I will. We want you to get better.

SADAKO

I want to get better, too! And I will. Soon.

TAKAMURA (to Kyushu)

You can relax for a second.

(The machine is pulled back and
wheeled out. Kyushu reclines on the
bed.)

SADAKO

Next year at graduation, I'll be at school. With everyone else.

OLDER BOY

We hope so.

FIRST GIRL

What do you mean, "hope so?"

(To Sadako:)

You'd <u>better</u> be there. Or we'll come down here and drag you out!

(The other children agree.)

FATHER

I'm sure your friends would like to stay longer....But Sadako needs to rest.

(Beginning to guide the children out.)

And I'm not sure she will, with all of us wanting to ask her questions.

SADAKO

Come back, though. It's lonely here.

OLDER BOY

We will.

(As they are leaving, the small boy lags behind. Sadako offers the bag of candy, and the boy returns to take one, smiles, and runs after the others. When they are gone, Sadako drops back onto the bed, tired. Her father returns.)

FATHER

I'll come back tomorrow.

SADAKO (without the energy she had)

Alright, father.

FATHER

Everything okay?

SADAKO (nodding)

I'm glad they came.

FATHER

There's an American doctor, who wants to talk to you...but I told her not today...you're tired. Sleep some.

SADAKO (wearily)

Alright....

(He kisses her forehead, watches her a moment, then exits. Dr. Takamura returns to Kyushu's bedside, studying a chart on a clipboard.)

KYUSHU

Well? What did you bring me?

TAKAMURA (preoccupied)

Hmm?

KYUSHU

Everyone's so happy. A day of...congratulations, celebrations. So?—What about me? Did you bring me any gifts?
(The physician stares at her.)

Any good news?

TAKAMURA (suddenly animated)
Oh yes! I almost forgot!...We're doing more tests tomorrow.
(Kyushu drops back on the bed
heavily.)
Isn't that what you wanted to hear?
(She throws up her hands to say "no.")
Let me ask you something. What do you notice, about your eyesight?

KYUSHU
What should I notice?

TAKAMURA
Do you see any shadows? Blurred vision or cloudiness?

KYUSHU
Did the machine tell you there was something wrong with my eyes?

TAKAMURA (shaking his head)
I can't say yet. I believe the results will show there has been some damage. But I think you could tell me more precisely what that damage is.
(Pause. Kyushu is silent, withdrawn.)
A lot of people were injured by looking at the bomb blast. Their eyes
were...burnt...and scarring occurred. Could that have happened to you?

KYUSHU
I don't see how. I wasn't in Hiroshima then.

TAKAMURA
You didn't see it?

KYUSHU
I wasn't anywhere near it.
(He considers arguing with her, decides against it.)

TAKAMURA (noting something on
chart)
I suppose...something else could have caused it then.

KYUSHU
Can you tell me what'll happen?

TAKAMURA (suddenly businesslike)
With what?

KYUSHU

My eyes!

TAKAMURA

Do you know what a cataract is?

KYUSHU

No—

TAKAMURA

Then it wouldn't do any good to explain it.

KYUSHU

But if you <u>explained</u> it, then I'd know.

TAKAMURA

And if you told me what you saw, then I'd know.
> (Pause. They've reached a stale-
> mate.)

It's too complicated. I don't have time. Concern yourself with getting stron-
ger.
> (Dr. Takamura exits. Kyushu pushes
> her hand through her hair, gazing
> straight ahead. Sadako stirs, watching
> the older girl, then climbs out of bed,
> carrying a chair and her candy to
> Kyushu's bed.)

SADAKO

They don't like to tell you much....Would you like some rice candy? It was
brought to me.

KYUSHU

No thanks.
> (Slight pause. Sadako unwraps a
> piece, eats it. Kyushu remains am-
> bivalent.)

You have a lot of friends.

SADAKO (concentrating on the candy)

Uh huh.

KYUSHU

How come they like you?

SADAKO

I don't know.

(Pause. Kyushu watches her eat.)

KYUSHU

Give me a piece of that candy.

SADAKO (handing it to her)

You can eat the wrapper too.

KYUSHU

Great.

(She puts it in her mouth.)

Why're you so cheerful? You like it in the hospital?

SADAKO

No, I'd rather be home. But it's not too bad. They show movies here!...And I don't plan to stay long.

KYUSHU

How's that?

SADAKO

I'm folding paper cranes.

KYUSHU (taking a second candy)

You're doing what?

SADAKO (handing Kyushu one)

You know. Origami. You take square sheets of paper, and fold them certain ways, and they make the shapes of different animals. They come in many colors, but for the cranes I think white is prettiest. Haven't you seen them?

KYUSHU

I guess I have. I just didn't know what they were.

SADAKO

They're supposed to bring good health.

KYUSHU (looks at it, unimpressed)

Oh, yeah. That should do it.

(Slight pause. She hands back the crane.)

20

SADAKO

It's not so bad though. Being here, for a little while.

KYUSHU

I guess it's okay if you've got friends bringing you gifts and things. Can I have one more piece?

SADAKO (holding open the bag)

Sure. They're good, huh?

(Kyushu nods, eating her third candy.)

KYUSHU

I don't plan to be here long either. I don't want to be here any longer than I have to.

SADAKO

What's wrong with you?

KYUSHU

They don't know. Soldiers brought me here, but the doctors don't know nothing ....What about you? You don't look sick. They told you what you got?

SADAKO

Uh-uh.

(She holds out the candy bag.)

KYUSHU (taking one, but not eating it)

I'll save one for later.

SADAKO

Are you afraid of getting genbakusho.

KYUSHU

Sure. Isn't everyone?

SADAKO

Are they?

KYUSHU (nodding)

A lot of people....You're too young to know about that. How old are you?

SADAKO

Twelve.

KYUSHU

That's too young to be afraid of diseases.

SADAKO

All my friends talk about it, though. We want to know what it is.
(Slight pause.)

KYUSHU

You can't get it. Not unless you were there when the A-bomb went off.

SADAKO

I heard people got it from just being around that part of the city afterwards.

KYUSHU

Where'd you hear that?

SADAKO

My father worked with some people who had genbakusho. They never
even knew it....They got sick, and they still are.
(Pause.)

KYUSHU

Well I know I don't have it.

SADAKO

How do you know?

KYUSHU

I'm too strong to be sick. And I was never there in the first place.

SADAKO

What're you doing in a hospital?

KYUSHU

I don't know! Maybe I'm some kind of political prisoner....Aren't you tired?
You should be in bed.

SADAKO

I'm not sleepy anymore.

                              KYUSHU
Well, I've got to get my rest. I can't spend all my time talking to sick people.
                              (Sadako returns to her bed. Slight
                              pause.)
What's your name?

                              SADAKO
Sadako. What's yours?

                              KYUSHU
Kyushu. Thanks for the candy.

                              SADAKO
You're welcome....Goodnight, Kyushu.

                              KYUSHU
Yeah.

                              (Kyushu lies there, but it's obvious she
                              isn't going to fall asleep, even as
                              Sadako rolls over and immediately
                              does.)

SCENE THREE

Early in the pre-dawn morning. Both Sadako and Kyushu are now sleeping. The Attendant enters in the dim light, approaches Sadako's bed. He quietly rummages through Sadako's things, until he finds something valuable. Kyushu wakes, watches him a moment.

KYUSHU

What do you got?

ATTENDANT (jumping)

Shh. Go back to sleep. It's too early to wake up.

KYUSHU (persisting)

What is it?

ATTENDANT (low, flustered)

What does it look like!...Keep it to yourself. Don't wake the whole ward.

KYUSHU

You're stealing that.

ATTENDANT

Stealing? From a little girl? I wouldn't do that. I was just...admiring it.

KYUSHU

Put it back.

ATTENDANT

You're getting pushy.

KYUSHU

She's sick! It's not fair to come in here and handle her things.

ATTENDANT (smiling)

Fair? Everything's fair. The world's upside-down, topsy-turvy. There aren't any rules anymore. Nobody knows what life is for because any minute they could drop that big one—Fat Boy's brother—and then what good would your

24

rules be? Flash! Boom! And it's all...over. What kind of life is that?

KYUSHU
People still have rights. We don't have to act like animals.

ATTENDANT
You don't have any rights <u>here</u>, you <u>are</u> animals—animals in a laboratory!...
Go to sleep, Sensai. So you can be alert. The Americans keep you alive to
have subjects for their lab tests. They'll feed you and pretend they care, as
long as you're a <u>good</u> animal. But when their tests are finished...they'll forget about us.

KYUSHU
Why would they do that?

ATTENDANT
They got to! It's research. They want to know about this radiation, so when
the Russians drop the big one on <u>them</u>, they'll know what to expect. Pretty
smart people, these Americans.
                                        (He smiles. Slight pause. His mood
                                        again shifts.)
You better get smart too, Sensai. I'm not going to keep this. I was only...
appreciating it. But if I wanted it, I could take it—and nobody would stop me
these days. Everyone is too busy looking out for themselves. And if you
want to survive, you better do the same.
                                        (He puts the object back where he got
                                        it, and exits. As he is leaving, he bows
                                        to the American doctor, who is enter-
                                        ing.)

                                        FRIZZEL (approaching Kyushu's bed)
Good morning, Kyushu.

                                        KYUSHU
Is it?

                                        FRIZZEL
It could be. Do you want to talk?

                                        KYUSHU (confrontationally)
Sure. Why are you here?

                                        (Dr. Frizzel gauges the girl's resent-
                                        ment.)

25

                                        FRIZZEL
It looks like we're back to square one.
                                        KYUSHU
I don't remember leaving it.

                                        FRIZZEL (nodding)
I guess we didn't.

                                        (Dr. Takamura enters.)

                                        TAKAMURA
Good morning.

                                        FRIZZEL
That's open for debate.

                                        (She exits.)

                                        TAKAMURA
You weren't cooperating.

                                        KYUSHU
I just want to get out of here, why do I have to answer all those questions?

                                        TAKAMURA
You answer the questions to help you get out of here.

                                        KYUSHU
I answer questions to help America win their Cold War with Russia.

                                        TAKAMURA
It is much too early for world affairs. Especially with someone who doesn't
know what she's talking about. Excuse me.
                                        (He leaves.)

                                        SADAKO
How are you today?

                                        KYUSHU
Tired.

                                        SADAKO
I'm tired too.

KYUSHU

Well, I'm tired of people pretending they care about me.

SADAKO

Did you sleep well?

KYUSHU

No!—How can I!...I woke up too early.

(Kyushu rubs her eyes, suddenly weary.)

SADAKO

Do your eyes bother you?

KYUSHU (amused by the question)

Yes, they do. They bother me with what they see, and they bother me with what they don't see.

(She becomes more serious.)

There was someone here this morning. Taking something. And I couldn't make out what it was. Just across the room. And I couldn't see it....I don't seem to be able to see anything the way it is.

SADAKO

I'm sorry, Kyushu. Did you tell the doctor?

KYUSHU

It's none of your business!...so don't be sorry, just...look out for yourself. Be careful, okay? Don't be so trusting.

(Dr. Frizzel returns to Kyushu's bedside, while the Nurse enters, rolling a wheelchair over to Sadako's bed.)

FRIZZEL

Let's start again.

KYUSHU

Is there any reason to?

FRIZZEL

I think so. We need to talk further.

NURSE (gently waking her)

Sadako-chan. The doctor says they must do further exams.

(She helps the weakened young girl out of her bed and into the wheelchair.)

FRIZZEL
Why won't you accept that the questions are for your own good?

NURSE (to Sadako)
Some tests may hurt, but they are for your good.

SADAKO
I know.
(She wheels Sadako out.)

KYUSHU
Where are they taking her?

FRIZZEL
To run some additional tests. They're going to the lab.

KYUSHU
The whole <u>place</u> is a lab! And I'm just a guinea pig, one more damn guinea pig in one of your experiments.

FRIZZEL
What gave you that idea?

KYUSHU
What's the difference? That's how I feel. You're wasting your time.
(Dr. Frizzel remains by Kyushu, but other scenes take place as though she had left.)

TAKAMURA (reentering, to Kyushu)
You're wasting time not talking to Dr. Frizzel. She could help you. And she's very persistent.

KYUSHU
Hasn't she asked enough questions already?

TAKAMURA
Not 'til we're satisfied you're healthy.
(He turns to exit, but also remains near the vicinity of Kyushu's bed.)

KYUSHU (calling after him)
If you'd leave me alone, I just might get better!

ATTENDANT (stepping in
surreptitiously)

You won't get better. Not with genbakusho.

(Sadako is wheeled into another part of
the room by the Nurse. Takamura
goes to her, and begins examining
her.)

FRIZZEL (to Kyushu)

Just how bad is your eyesight?

KYUSHU

You don't give up, do you?

FRIZZEL

No, I hope I'm every bit as stubborn as you are.

(Slight pause. Kyushu tries to see
what Takamura is doing with Sadako.)

KYUSHU (referring to Takamura)

What did he tell you?

FRIZZEL

He said you were as stubborn as I was. I told him I doubted it.

(The Attendant pulls a large hospital
partition into place, masking the actions of Takamura—but in so doing ex-
poses a scene of burnt wreckage from
the Hiroshima bomb blast. Only
Kyushu is aware of it. She hesitates
when she sees it.)

KYUSHU (uncomfortably)

Did he...say I wouldn't talk to him either?

FRIZZEL

Yes....

(What Kyushu sees is a stone portal,
with twisted metal and debris tumbled
around it. Smoke swirls about, partly
concealing a figure lying across the
threshold.)

What did he want to know?

FIGURE IN PORTAL (not clearly
visible)

Mizu...

29

KYUSHU

Dr. Takamura...asked about my eyes. I couldn't tell him what I saw...
because some of it's...in my imagination.

FRIZZEL

How do you know?

FIGURE IN PORTAL (gently stirring)

Mizu...

KYUSHU

It's from the past. Something I...remembered.

FRIZZEL

Do you want to describe it to me?

FIGURE IN PORTAL (pushing itself up)

Mizu...

KYUSHU

No. I don't think I want to.

(Pause. There is no movement anywhere.)

FRIZZEL

That's fine. We'll stick to more concrete things. Why did you decide to talk
to me now, Kyushu?

KYUSHU

Because I'm afraid.

FRIZZEL

About your vision?

KYUSHU

Yeah....That's part of it. Do you think I could lose my sight?

FRIZZEL (carefully)

You've already experienced a slight diminution of—

KYUSHU

Doctor!—Don't dance around with big words; if I wanted to hear that, I could
talk to him....I could still lose all of it, right?...I could go blind?

FRIZZEL

Dr. Takamura will work very hard to avoid that. But yes, you could.

KYUSHU

Completely blind.

FRIZZEL

As I understand it, it depends on how much damage has been done to the posterior lens, and the lens fibers.
(She smiles gently.)
Sorry. Dr. Takamura's the expert. I can only repeat what he told me.
(Slight pause.)

KYUSHU

And they don't know yet? About the damage?

FRIZZEL

Not yet.
(Slight pause. The Figure stirs again.)

KYUSHU

That's all though.

FRIZZEL

What do you mean?

KYUSHU

My eyes. That's all they've found wrong.

FRIZZEL

That's...an odd question. For most people, that would be enough.

KYUSHU

Well, sure—I don't want to be blind!—it's a scary thought....But there are worse things...than not being able to see.

FIGURE IN PORTAL
(Still not identifiable)

Mizu...

FRIZZEL

Like what?

31

                              KYUSHU (simply stated)
Like dying.

                              FIGURE IN PORTAL
Dozo....Mizu-wo sukoshi kudasai. [Please....Give me some water.]
                              (Pause.)

                              KYUSHU (ignoring the Figure)
They don't think...I have A-bomb illness?

                              FRIZZEL
Is there any reason to suspect you would?

                              KYUSHU
No.

                              FRIZZEL
Then why do you ask?

                              KYUSHU
It's just...so many people here have it....Isn't that what this hospital's for?

                              FRIZZEL (slowly)
It's true. Most of our patients have injuries...illnesses...related to the bomb,
in one way or another. And we don't know yet, Kyushu, about you. That's
why we take all the tests, and ask all the questions.
                              (Slight pause. She studies Kyushu's
                              face.)
But if what you say is true, about not having been in Hiroshima, you should
have less to worry about than the others.

                              FIGURE IN PORTAL (plaintively)
Mizu!

                              (The Figure rises up, freeing itself from
                              the debris, and revealing itself to be
                              the Cockroach woman. She stands
                              among the wreckage, showing mimeti-
                              cally that she is very thirsty.)

                              KYUSHU (frightened, losing her
                              resolve)
I was in Hiroshima—

                              (The Cockroach woman reaches to-
                              wards Kyushu, hands and arms pain-
                              fully burnt.)

                              32

COCKROACH WOMAN (desperately)

Mizu—

KYUSHU

After the bomb blast. And I did see it. Would that change things?

FRIZZEL

That depends.

KYUSHU

On what?

FRIZZEL

On how long you were there. And how soon after the blast.
(Slight pause. Kyushu considers this.)
What are you thinking about? Is there something you're afraid to tell me?

KYUSHU

I'm not afraid. I'll tell you everything. What do you want to know?

FRIZZEI

What else did you see?

KYUSHU

I saw bodies. Blackened by fire. Dead...people. Walking about. I couldn't
understand, I was five years old, how could dead people be walking? But
something had happened, the world had changed. The whole world was on
fire. People ran everywhere, yelling for "water, water, to put out the fires."
They were all around us. And smoke. And stink. And those dead people,
with their hands stretched out,...some of them with strips of skin, hanging
like black ribbons...calling for "water...water..."
(The Cockroach woman takes a step
nearer and Kyushu responds excit-
edly.)
And I ran to my house, but it was on fire! I called for my parents. Nobody
answered! Just people, running crazy, place to place,—looking for friends
or someone familiar; running for help and news of their families; running
from the dead with their hands outstretched; running from the flames with
the whole world on fire!—"Mizu! Mizu! Please give me water."
(The Cockroach woman moves for-
ward a shuffling step, her hands still
reaching for Kyushu. Kyushu watches
her, but grows more calm.)

33

KYUSHU (continuing)
Someone knocked me down. I was frightened, I was crying. But more than anything, I hated the Americans, even though I'd never met any. I hated you for burning my house. For taking my parents. For leaving me alone, in a bombed-out city. A "furo-ji": An orphan. Begging for money from American soldiers. G.I. Joes who laugh at you and call you the Tokio Kid. I'd never seen Tokyo!—they didn't know. A Jap was a Jap; and a chocolate bar made everything O-K....I don't know how I grew up, but I did—haunted by those American faces,...by the buildings no one would tear down or repair,...by the dead you'd set loose to walk on the streets, which was where I lived....

COCKROACH WOMAN (advancing a step)

Mizu?

KYUSHU (growing more agitated)
And soon I decided I didn't want to see anymore!...Then suddenly, the worst thing was...that I stopped. Things became fuzzy, indistinct. I couldn't see faces—they were blurred, smudged out. Again I became frightened, and I hated you more—because even when I thought that this might be better, that this might be alright,...I realized I could still hear your voices—asking me questions, calling me names,—

COCKROACH WOMAN
Tasukete kure! Mizu! [Please help me! Water!]

KYUSHU
—pleading for water I didn't have! Why won't you leave me alone?—Why won't you leave me alone!—Why won't you leave me alone!
(Kyushu collapses, burying herself in the bedding. Pause. The Attendant replaces the hospital partition, masking the portal and the Cockroach woman. Takamura and the Nurse come to Kyushu's bedside. He applies some drops to Kyushu's eyes, and wraps a large gauze bandage around her head, completely covering her eyes. The hospital staff quietly exit.)

SADAKO
I feel better now. I slept.

(Silence. Sadako goes to Kyushu.)

How are your eyes, Kyushu?

KYUSHU (with comical simplicity)

They itch.

SADAKO

Is the medicine helping?

KYUSHU

I'm not sure....I can't see anything with this bandage on.
(Slight pause.)

SADAKO (grabbing it enthusiastically)

My father brought me a book! Would you like to—
(As she runs over to Kyushu's bed with
it, she remembers her friend can't see
it.)

Oh....Sorry.

KYUSHU (taking the book)

No, that's okay, I can always feel the pictures. What's it about?

SADAKO

Origami animals. It shows how to fold twenty-five different kinds.

KYUSHU (smiling)

By the time you get out of here, you'll have made a zoo

SADAKO

No, I'm only making the cranes. The "Orizuru."

KYUSHU

They have their own name, hah?

SADAKO

Uh-huh....You can look at this tomorrow.
(She takes book from Kyushu's
hands.)

KYUSHU

Yeah.
(Slight pause.)
Have you made any more..."Orizuru?"

SADAKO

Oh, yes! A lot.

KYUSHU

When will you stop with them?

SADAKO (with some pride)

When I've folded one thousand.

KYUSHU (suddenly laughing)

A thousand! Why so many?

SADAKO

It's a tradition! Since the crane is believed to live a thousand years, anyone who folds one thousand paper cranes will have a long and healthy life.

KYUSHU

And you wish to be healthy?

SADAKO

Not just me—everybody. No more illness. No more genbakusho. If everyone was healthy, they might be happy. And then maybe there wouldn't be so much fighting either.

KYUSHU (touched by her innocence)

That's one way of looking at it....A good way.
(Slight pause.)

SADAKO

Would you like me to show you how to make them?

KYUSHU (smiling)

That would be difficult. Maybe tomorrow.

SADAKO (running back for a paper)

You don't need your eyes for this, Kyushu, just your hands! You just have to be able to feel the paper.
(She gets an origami crane that's al
ready half finished, and gently places
Kyushu's fingers on it, guiding her.)
Okay. Here's one I've already started. We fold here and here...bend this back...this makes the wings...and this is the neck and head. Finished!

KYUSHU

How does it look?

SADAKO (holding it out proudly)

It's very pretty, Kyushu. A delicate white crane.
(Kyushu smiles at the crane she cannot see. Sadako places it in Kyushu's cupped hands, and lifts them up, to display the beautiful white crane.)

We can write "peace" on your wings,...and you will fly all over the world.
(The two girls are isolated in white light as **Act One** ends.)

SCENE FOUR

As Act Two begins, the schoolchildren
are seated in a semicircle, watching as
Takamura carefully removes Kyushu's
bandage. Her eyes are shut; she's
afraid to open them but does so, cautiously.

TAKAMURA

Well?

KYUSHU (squinting into medical lamp)

The light is so bright.

TAKAMURA (looking in her eyes)

It will seem so for awhile.
(He smiles, turning out the lamp.)
But in fact, it's the same light we had when we put the bandages on....I
want you to take it easy today. Don't run to the window, to watch the sun
set. And do not rub your eyes. If they burn or feel irritated, let the attendant
know, we'll put some drops in.
(Kyushu blinks, her eyesight adjusting.)
Are you getting used to it?

KYUSHU

Slowly.

(She glances around the room. Pause.
The children rise formally and exit.)

TAKAMURA (collecting his things)

You were pretty hard on Dr. Frizzel.

KYUSHU (preoccupied with her sight)

She was pretty hard on me.

TAKAMURA

Why don't you like her?

KYUSHU

Am I supposed to like her?

(Before he can respond)

She's American—Do you like her?

(Pause.)

38

TAKAMURA

I don't have to. She is a guest of our government, doing important work—

KYUSHU

Important to who?

TAKAMURA (simply)

Important to her. Important to Japan. And most important to you.

KYUSHU (to herself)

Important to the Americans.

(Slight pause)

TAKAMURA

You may not like them being here. I don't, not when it affects my work. But they are here, and we should show them we can be...courteous. If she comes in today, will you talk to her?

KYUSHU (without conviction)

You're the doctor.

TAKAMURA

That's true. And for my prescription, I ask you to be as friendly as possible.
(He exits. Kyushu hops out of bed to visit Sadako. The Nurse is at Sadako's bed-side, straightening things up.)

KYUSHU

Good morning!

SADAKO (sleepily)

Good morning, Kyushu. They took your bandages off.

KYUSHU

Yep!

SADAKO

How do you feel today?

KYUSHU

Much better. But I think maybe Dr. Takamura woke up on the wrong side of the bed.

SADAKO

How can you tell that?

KYUSHU

It's something Americans say. Means he's in a bad mood....What do you think of him?

SADAKO

I like him.

KYUSHU

How come?

SADAKO

I don't know. I just think he really cares if people get better....Did he say anything about surgery?

KYUSHU

Neh, nothing yet. He's letting my eyes rest awhile before checking them. But they feel fine!...What about the American? You like her too?

SADAKO (nodding)

She's nice. She listens.

KYUSHU (dismissing it with a face)

That's her job.

SADAKO

Yes. But some people do it better than others.

KYUSHU (thinking it over)

Maybe I'll give her another chance.

(Slight pause. The Nurse helps Sadako into a hospital wheelchair.)

SADAKO

I don't think it's fair!

KYUSHU

What's not?

SADAKO

That you're better, after folding one crane,—and I've still got over three hundred to go!

KYUSHU

I'm not better yet!

SADAKO

You look better than I do.

(She smiles.)

KYUSHU

You'll finish them. And I'll still be moping around here, complaining.

SADAKO (sighing)

I know....But it won't be today.

(The Nurse begins pushing the girl out.)

KYUSHU

Where're you going now?

SADAKO

Where else? More tests.

(Sadako and the Nurse roll out of view.)

KYUSHU (calling after Sadako)

Again?...Is that all they do here?

(Dr. Frizzel has entered, and sits at Kyushu's bedside, engaged in a conversation that has clearly started.)

FRIZZEL (writing on her clipboard)

The tests are designed to see if you're improving.

KYUSHU

Can't you tell I'm improving. I thought I was much more "cooperative" today.

(Dr. Frizzel smiles to herself.)

What are you smiling at?

FRIZZEL

Oh,...I'm just happy you're in a better frame of mind.

KYUSHU

Good! I'm happy you're happy.

FRIZZEL

Yes....Well, I'm glad to hear that. And I wanted to find out how you were feeling now.

KYUSHU

Can't you see? I'm feeling great. My eyes feel good, and I'm much more rested.

FRIZZEL (carefully)

Sometimes people can look great on the outside, and not be well on the inside.

(Silence.)

I just want to make sure we've helped you,...in any way we can. Have you thought about our conversation?

KYUSHU

Not a lot.

FRIZZEL

Have you thought of anything else you'd like to tell me? Anything else you remember?

KYUSHU

No. I told you everything.

FRIZZEL

Are you sure?

(Slight pause.)

KYUSHU

What do you remember, doctor?

FRIZZEL

What do you mean?

KYUSHU

What do you remember, from when you were five? What things come to mind?

42

FRIZZEL

Mainly I remember being with my family.

KYUSHU

Was it a large family?

(Slight pause. Dr. Frizzel is
consciously going along with Kyushu's
questioning.)

FRIZZEL

I had two sisters and a younger brother; my mother's sister lived with us,
and my grandparents were nearby. I guess you'd say it was a large family
at holidays.

KYUSHU

And what would you do at your holidays?

FRIZZEL

We'd celebrate with a special dinner. And after we ate, my father would
read to us, then he and my grandfather would play a card game called crib-
bage. Later, we'd all sing around the piano.

KYUSHU

What's a piano?

FRIZZEL

A musical instrument. Very pretty. My mother taught people to play it.

KYUSHU

Did she teach you?

FRIZZEL (smiling)

She tried. But I didn't have any aptitude—

(Realizing this word is above Kyushu.)

—any ear for music. I preferred reading. My oldest sister did play profes-
sionally, though.

KYUSHU

She doesn't play anymore?

FRIZZEL

She died a few years ago.

(Slight pause.)

                              KYUSHU
And the rest of your family?

                              FRIZZEL
My parents still live in Connecticut, but my aunt and grandparents are gone.
My younger sister's married, in nearby New Hampshire. And my brother
was killed in the war.

                              KYUSHU
Fighting Japan?

                              FRIZZEL
No. In Europe.

                              (She pauses, and tries to smile, but
                              she's inadvertently touched some deep
                              losses.)
It seems like a long time ago.

                              KYUSHU
You still remember those early days though.

                              FRIZZEL
Certainly I do. I remember them very fondly.

                              KYUSHU
Well I don't, doctor. Everything that happened before the bomb was burnt
away by the explosion, and everything that happened afterwards I've told
you about. I don't say this to be difficult. I just want to explain. For me, the
past has been horrible—but it is the past. I feel good now, healthier. I don't
want to look back at the horrors. I want to look ahead.

                              (A JAPANESE WOMAN enters with
                              her son. He is the small boy from
                              Sadako's group of schoolfriends.
                              They approach the American doctor
                              hesitantly.)

                              JAPANESE WOMAN (in halting
                              English)
Pardon me, lady-san, I thought we'd find Sadako Sasake here.

                              SMALL BOY (pointing to Sadako's
                              bed)
She was over there.

                              JAPANESE WOMAN
Hush, Matsuo. Let the American lady speak.

                                44

                              FRIZZEL
Your son's right, that is her bed. But they've taken her to the lab.

                              JAPANESE WOMAN
Is she alright?

                              FRIZZEL (nodding)
They're running tests.
                              (The Woman looks confused.)

                              SMALL BOY (explaining)
To see if she is better.

                              JAPANESE WOMAN (understanding)
We brought her some things, wrapped in this furoshiki [square cloth].
                              (She holds up an attractive bundle.)
A hair brush, pens and paper—things we thought she'd like.

                              FRIZZEL
I'm sure she will. Why don't you leave them on the bed, and I'll take you to
someone who can find Dr. Takamura.

                              JAPANESE WOMAN
Thank you, lady-san.
                              (She bows, and hands the bundle to
                              her son, quietly telling him to wait
                              there.)

                              FRIZZEL (to Kyushu)
I'm very glad you're improving, Kyushu. But this is only the first day. And,
in my field, what you think, and what you imagine, is every bit as important
to health as how you feel. For many survivors, there are feelings—terrible
feelings of guilt or fear—that remain with them, haunting them for years. To
really recover—to look ahead, as you say—you have to face those fears.
They can't be ignored.

                              KYUSHU (subdued)
What would I feel guilty about?

                              FRIZZEL
I don't know, unless you tell me.
                              (Slight pause. Kyushu doesn't
                              respond.)
I'll come back later.

                              45

                                    (Dr. Frizzel joins the Japanese woman
                                    and they exit together.)

                                    KYUSHU (to herself)
I can't wait.

                                    (The small boy sets down the furoshiki
                                    and sits in a chair next to Sadako's
bed,   watching Kyushu. Eventually, she
                                    notices him staring at her.)
Don't you think you should go with your mother?
                                    (The boy shakes his head, staring.)
Are you just going to sit there, watching me?
                                    (He again shakes his head, but
                                    continues to stare.)
Then why are you doing it!
                                    (Slight pause.)

                                    SMALL BOY
Where are your scars?

                                    KYUSHU
My what?

                                    SMALL BOY
Your burn scars. From the bomb. Aren't you a hibakusha?

                                    KYUSHU
No. I'm a leper.

                                    (She has pulled one arm into her
                                    pajama sleeve without his noticing,
                                    concealing it, preparing to play a joke
                                    on him.)

                                    SMALL BOY (shocked, wide-eyed)
Lie! Soo-de suka? [No! Is that so?]

                                    KYUSHU
Sure. If you look here...in my sleeve...you can see where my arm...*fell off.*
                                    (He reluctantly walks over to Kyushu's
                                    bed. As he peeks into the limp
                                    sleeve, she shoots out her hand, grabs
                                    his face.)
Boo!

(The boy yells, runs out after his mother. Kyushu laughs, but it doesn't last. The hospital is now too quiet. She goes to Sadako's bed. She picks up the Origami book, meanders slowly back to her own bed. The Attendant enters with a rolling laundry hamper, unnoticed by Kyushu, who climbs back onto her bed, to look through Sadako's book. She seems easily distracted by the silence around her, but tries to occupy herself with the pictures.)

COCKROACH WOMAN'S VOICE

Mizu....

(Kyushu stops, and looks around, but the nightmare figure is not visible. Pause.)

Mizu....

(She tries to ignore the voice by paying even closer attention to the book. The Attendant takes a sheet from the hamper and puts it over his head. Then he sneaks up behind Kyushu, like a spectre.)

ATTENDANT (in a deliberately eerie voice)

Urameshiya....

(Kyushu jumps at the sound, then, seeing him, pulls the sheet off him. He laughs.)

What's the matter—did I frighten you? You look like you saw a "ghost."

KYUSHU (looking around for a source)

No. Only <u>heard</u> one.

ATTENDANT (nodding)

Hospitals can be spooky places. Sometimes I come in late, after the patients are asleep, and I can see those tiny blue flames the ancient ones say are our spirits—rising up from the bodies as they lay in the dark.

(He shivers at the memory, having fun.)

These poor unknowing "gisei," these scapegoats, laying there with their souls—or maybe radiation!—<u>floating</u> away, into the darkness....<u>Very</u> bukimi [ghastly].

(He smiles, as though his story has clearly carried some great significance. Pause.)

47

                              KYUSHU (marginally interested)
Have you ever seen a ghost, any of those nights.

                              ATTENDANT (hesitates, thinking)
No. No ghosts. Only the flames. Rising up, floating away, on the
"MujoKaze," the "wind of change...."
                              (Kyushu has returned to the book.)
You don't like my poetry, Sensai?

                              (Kyushu snorts, shrugging her
                              shoulders, ignoring the presence of the
                              Attendant.)
Have <u>you</u> seen a ghost?

                              KYUSHU (rising to the challenge)
I've seen things...that would turn your hair white, and stand it on end.

                              ATTENDANT (laughing, begins to
                              sweep)
Tell me sometime, Sensai! I'd like a story like that, to tell other patients.
They enjoy spooky stories, late at night. You tell me, heh?

                              KYUSHU
Come back tomorrow, I'll tell you all about it.

                              ATTENDANT
What's the matter? You're unhappy today?

                              KYUSHU (looking at the book)
I'm <u>very</u> happy today.

                              ATTENDANT
You have a funny way of showing it.
                              (She doesn't respond, continuing to
                              read. As he becomes aware of the
                              book:)
Oh, so! No <u>wonder</u> you're happy. Someone else has a...light touch!
                              (He grabs the book from her hands.)

                              KYUSHU
Hey! What're you doing?

                              ATTENDANT (holding the book away)
What are <u>you</u> doing? Stealing a book from a little girl?—a <u>sick</u> little girl?
What a terrible thing!
                              (Kyushu tries to take it back from him.)

48

KYUSHU

I'm not a thief!

ATTENDANT (teasing her with it)

Is this your book?

KYUSHU (chasing him)

Give it back!

ATTENDANT (avoiding her)

It's alright, Sensai!—I won't tell anyone! These are hard times.
> (He stops, tosses the book back to her.)

After the war, when I first came to Hiroshima, people were very desperate. Some could be seen squatting in burnt-down houses, sifting ashes through their fingers, to find a couple yen or jewelry they could sell. Others I heard of actually cut rings and watches off the bodies of victims. Terrible times, Sensai. But I understand.
> (He moves closer, confidently.)

I understand you, Sensai. A furo-ji. An A bomb orphan. You lived in that world, didn't you? I'll bet you stole things, hid from police? Terrible hard times, eh?...
> (Kyushu is silent. The Attendant smiles, goes to her bed and lies down familiarly.)

People don't have to be that desperate. They just need to help each other a little. I give you a hand; you give me a hand.

KYUSHU (suspiciously)

How can I help you?

ATTENDANT

That little girl likes you. You're kind to her, you talk to her, that's nice. Her father is concerned—he wants her to have a friend in the hospital, so maybe she won't be frightened. He's thankful when she finds one. He's also very generous: Brings you a present—possibly brings you two! You say, "lie [no,] that's okay, I don't want any gifts!"....But if it's something   of value, I sell it for you! And then we split the money.
> (Attendant swings his legs off the bed.)

See how that works? Little girl has a friend; father feels satisfied. I help you; you help me. That way, everybody feels good. Everybody helps everybody.

KYUSHU (slowly)

The only thing...I'd like to help you do...is find the door out of here.

ATTENDANT (suddenly dour)
Don't act high-and-mighty with me, you're not so special. And what's wrong
with being a friend to a poor sick little girl? Are you ashamed?

KYUSHU
Nothing's wrong with it. I just don't think she should have to pay for it.

ATTENDANT
It won't make any difference to her! She's not going to live much longer
anyway.

KYUSHU
Don't you say that anymore!

ATTENDANT (simply)
It's true.

KYUSHU
It isn't either! She's not that sick!—And she's getting better!
(Pause. The Attendant appears
genuinely concerned for Kyushu for the
first time.)

ATTENDANT (quietly)
Who told you that?...I'm sorry, Sensai, I don't say this to upset you. But she
is a very sick little girl.
(The Nurse, wearing medical gloves
and a mask, slowly pushes Sadako in
on a large hospital gurney. The small
girl climbs weakly from the one bed to
the other.)

ATTENDANT (confidentially, to
Kyushu)
Ask the doctors. They know. I heard them talking about her.
(He scampers to Sadako's bedside,
and covers her with a sheet, before
leaving. Slight pause. Kyushu goes to
Sadako.)

KYUSHU (quietly)
How are you feeling now?

SADAKO
Very tired. From someone as small as me...I don't think they should take so
much blood. Somebody should tell them....

50

KYUSHU

I'll talk to the doctor.

SADAKO

I just wish I could get some rest. Do you ever get so tired you can't fall asleep?

KYUSHU

No. Sometimes I <u>worry</u> so much it keeps me awake,—

SADAKO

Poor Kyushu. Are you worried about your eyes? They look a little red.

KYUSHU

Are they? I guess...I thought I was better sooner than I should have.

SADAKO

You'll be okay.

KYUSHU

Sure. Why wouldn't I?...Would you like something to drink?

SADAKO

No, my throat's too dry. I don't even want to swallow water!
                    (She smiles. Pause.)

KYUSHU

Doesn't it frighten you...that you could die here?

SADAKO

It <u>would</u>, I guess.

KYUSHU (prompting her to finish)

But?

SADAKO (smiling)

I don't think about dying. I think about going home.
                    (Kyushu nods.)
Do you know what I miss most? Sweet potatoes. My mother makes very good sweet potatoes...When you talk to the doctor, tell him that's what I want.

KYUSHU

Okay. Would you like some help, folding your cranes?

SADAKO

No. Not right now. It's funny. I think I'm ready...to fall asleep after all. Goodnight, Kyushu.

KYUSHU

Yeah. Well, sleep well.

(The Nurse pulls over a white hospital partition, effectively masking the bed from Kyushu's view. Takamura enters wearily, also in surgical scrubs, and slowly removes his mask and gloves.)

TAKAMURA (aware of Kyushu)

You wish to speak to me?

KYUSHU

I wanted to ask you some questions.

TAKAMURA

About your eyesight?

KYUSHU

No. About Sadako.

TAKAMURA

I see....What did you want to know?

KYUSHU

You keep taking tests.

TAKAMURA (showing his fatigue)

Yes. Test after test.

KYUSHU (persisting)

Is that because she's healthier?

TAKAMURA

I couldn't say. In this instance....She's a difficult case, I'm not sure I can explain it.

KYUSHU

That's what you said about my eyes! Okay, maybe I won't understand. <u>Talk</u> to me anyway.

TAKAMURA (frustrated)

Do you think I have time to stop and discuss every—

KYUSHU

I want to know!

TAKAMURA

Why? It doesn't have anything to do with your situation.

KYUSHU

She's my friend!

TAKAMURA (reverting to his old MO)

The tests indicated the development of certain neoplasia, and an increased number of leukocytes in the bloodstream,—

KYUSHU (interrupting him)

Dr. Takamura, <u>please</u>! No fancy medical words. Just tell me what's wrong with her.

(Takamura's energy visibly leaves him. He is disarmed and exhausted.)

TAKAMURA

"Karada ga darui." The body...is weary. Her strength is...simply gone.... Why do you look at me like that?

KYUSHU

I'm...surprised. I've never heard you use a Japanese expression before.
(Slight pause.)
Have you talked to her?

TAKAMURA

About what?

KYUSHU

Her illness.

TAKAMURA

I haven't told her anything! And I shouldn't be telling you!

KYUSHU

Why haven't you talked to her, if you already knew—?

TAKAMURA

Because I didn't want to admit ...

KYUSHU

How sick she was?

(He doesn't respond. Slight pause.)

Is she going to die?

TAKAMURA

I can't discuss this any further—

KYUSHU

She's a helpless little girl!

TAKAMURA

I won't discuss this with you!—Such things are confidential! Now pardon me.

(He exits quickly, troubled by Kyushu's questions. Kyushu moves back to her bed. In the center of the room, two partitions are drawn together to form a large blank screen. Other patients enter the room, accompanied by the Nurse and Attendant. The lights inside the hospital are dimmed. A silent movie is shown for the patients. Kyushu watches the film from her bed, and is lit by the projection beam. Laughter is heard from the other viewers of the film, but Kyushu is silent. Throughout, Sadako's bed is noticeably empty. As the film ends, the hospital room goes completely dark.)

SCENE FIVE

Dr. Frizzel is seated at Kyushu's bed-side. Her questions are interrupted by other character's exchanges with Kyushu, but not effected by them; they are separate.

FRIZZEL

What have you been thinking about?

KYUSHU

How quiet it is.

ATTENDANT (whispering, from a corner)

I saw Sadako last night.

FRIZZEL

You haven't been resting.

KYUSHU

No. I lay awake a lot.

ATTENDANT (begins scrubbing the floor)

I waved my hand. I don't think she saw me.

FRIZZEL

Did you like the movie last week?

KYUSHU

It was okay.

FRIZZEL

You didn't think it was funny?

KYUSHU

I guess it was. Until the end.

FRIZZEL

What didn't you like about the ending?

KYUSHU (petulantly)

I didn't say I didn't like it!...It was just sad.

FRIZZEL

Do you think so?

KYUSHU

Sure!

FRIZZEL

Why?

KYUSHU

It was sad!—It was hopeless!

(Dr. Frizzel writes on her clipboard.)

ATTENDANT (as he scrubs, on his
knees)

They have her in a private ward, where everyone's hooked up to blood. They're trying to put life back in her.

KYUSHU (whispering back, harshly)

She'll be all right!

ATTENDANT (shaking his head)

She doesn't look good, Sensai.

TAKAMURA (entering, with charts)

You don't look as good this week. There's a localized opacity on the anterior capsule, and your visual acuity was below what I expected....Would you like me to explain that, Kyushu?

KYUSHU (laying back in bed)

No. What difference will it make?

TAKAMURA

Unless you talk to me, it's hard to know how to help you.

KYUSHU

Now you want to talk. What can I tell you you don't already know?

TAKAMURA

Why you're giving up.

KYUSHU (turning to the doctor)

It's sad! It's hopeless!

56

FRIZZEL (conversationally)
I would've thought you'd like Charlie Chaplin. A lot of people did, after the war. Laughter's good medicine, according to several studies. But people also identify with him as the "little man," struggling against a world that—

KYUSHU (interrupting her)
Those must be people who lived. The dead ones aren't laughing much.

ATTENDANT
Nobody laughs up there. The whole ward...is completely...silent.

JAPANESE WOMAN (reentering with son)
Pardon. I thought we'd find Sadako Sasake here.

KYUSHU (confidentially, to Attendant)
Did she say anything to you?

ATTENDANI
No. Nobody talks, nobody laughs. Very bukimi.
(The Attendant exits. Dr. Frizzel remains bent over her clipboard.)

KYUSHU (calling after the Attendant)
Tell her to get better!

TAKAMURA
Don't you want to get better?

SMALL BOY
Aren't you a hibakusha?

TAKAMURA
Where's your resolve?

SMALL BOY
Where are your scars?

JAPANESE WOMAN
Where is Sadako Sasake?

KYUSHU (angrily, to Dr. Frizzel)
It's just too damn late!

(The Japanese woman and her son
exit.
All other movement in the hospital
stops, as Kyushu regains her
equilibrium:)
At the end of the movie, the girl has her eyesight and her hope, sure—but
what's happened to the man who helped restore it? The world...has ruined
him. It shows in his face, as he hides behind the flower she gave him. He'll
never be the same. Not now. And they'll never be together.
(Silence.)
Unless they can help him too, it's too late.
(Sadako appears separately, brought
in by her Father, pushing her in the
wheelchair. She looks small and
weak.)

TAKAMURA
We can try surgery. A partial epilation may improve your sight. Would you
like me to tell you what that is?

KYUSHU
It doesn't make any difference, I'm not getting better.

TAKAMURA (forcefully)
You'll see more <u>clearly</u>.

KYUSHU
What's there to see?—if I only live a week, or a month?

TAKAMURA
You can't <u>expect</u> not to live.

KYUSHU
No? Why not?

TAKAMURA (turning to leave)
Because I believe we can help you!

KYUSHU (calling to him as he goes)
Like Sadako?
(He is gone, but Kyushu yells after him.)
Do you build up her hopes, too?—for nothing?

FRIZZEL
A <u>life</u> is something.

KYUSHU

How long, though? How <u>long</u> a life?...If you can assure me she'll get better ...then I'll believe you. I'll believe you.

> (The Attendant reenters, and goes quietly to Sadako's bed. He methodically strips it of its bedding, as Kyushu and Frizzel watch.)

KYUSHU (to the Attendant)

What are you doing?

> (He freezes, very much as though he has been caught at something.)

ATTENDANT (to Frizzel)

Excuse me, Doctor. I didn't mean to interrupt.

> (He resumes his task, piling the bedding and pillows on top of the mattress.)

KYUSHU

Why are you <u>doing</u> that?

> ATTENDANT (stopping, non-plussed)

I'm sorry. I'm just...changing the bed clothes.

> (He bundles them together, in a hurry, while trying to avoid Kyushu's eyes.)

I won't be long.

KYUSHU

Where are the new sheets? How are you going to make the bed?

> (The Attendant scoops up the bedding.)

What happens when she comes back?

> (Pause. The Attendant stands silently, holding the bedding and looking down. He slowly looks up to face Kyushu.)

ATTENDANT

She won't be back, Sensai. Not now. Somethings...can't <u>come</u> back.

> (Slight pause.)

She was very brave, with her Papa-san standing there holding her hand.

> (Sadako's Father does this, then exits.)

And when he would leave, she'd fold the origami papers, making little birds, one after another—like they could still make things better for her.

59

SADAKO (cupping her hands under
an imaginary crane)
We'll write "peace" on your wings, and you'll fly all over the world.
(Sadako opens her hands, releasing
the imagined crane to fly.)

ATTENDANT
But she was too small. She wasn't strong enough to survive the A-bomb
sickness. Nobody is.
(Sadako's arms slowly drop, as does
her face. The Nurse enters, to take
her off.)
Once you have the genbakusho,...your life is over.
(The Attendant carries the bedding to
the edge of the hospital area, but
remains.)

FRIZZEL (carefully)
A little girl died....And we all feel bad about it, we can't help that....But it
doesn't mean you're going to die.

KYUSHU (quietly)
Once you have genbakusho,—

FRIZZEL (with persistence and conviction)
Sadako didn't die of "genbakusho," she died of leukemia—a disease that
can be seen and diagnosed. And you don't have it.

KYUSHU (desperate)
Sadako didn't look sick either. You could see she was getting better—just
by looking at her.

FRIZZEL
You wanted to see that, Kyushu, but she was very sick. She'd gotten
weaker since she came here. You just couldn't see what was happening
inside her.

KYUSHU
And you can't see what's inside me! What the bomb did to my body can't
be seen. I was there—I was exposed to the radiation. I'm a hibakusha; I
always will be.

FRIZZEL
But what does it mean to be a "hibakusha," Kyushu? That you're a victim?
(She clasps Kyushu's hands in hers.)

60

FRIZZEL (continuing)

Yes, it can mean that. But it also means you're a survivor: You have lived through the worst catastrophe—the worst *madness* —man could create. And yet, you survived.

(Slight pause. She gathers her strength.)

Other people didn't survive and that's hard to accept. You can't understand why you lived and they didn't, it doesn't seem fair. But you have to accept it, you have to go on with your life....That requires two very difficult things, however. First, you have to accept what's happened to you. You won't ever make sense out of your survival if you're trying to forget what you've been through....And when you've accepted the past, as part of who you are, then you have to move beyond it. You have to start living again, with some sort of purpose, and not be afraid!...

(She gently releases Kyushu's hands. Her intensity has come from something personal and emotional—not "clinical.")

It's not the bomb that's killing you now, Kyushu. It's fear.

(Dr. Frizzel waits, but Kyushu is silent. The doctor rises to leave)

KYUSHU

What...frightens you? Aren't you afraid?

FRIZZEL

Yes, I am. I'm afraid of death. Of losing my husband, or my little girl. Of losing my parents. It frightens me that I live in a world where we could lose loved ones so suddenly. But this makes me want to live very much, Kyushu. I want my life with them to...have meaning, I suppose.

(Slight pause.)

But even if I lost my husband or my little girl, I'd still want to go on, I'd want to live as long as I could,...to remember them, as long as I could. Just as you'll want to remember your friendship with Sadako.

(She hesitates.)

Can I tell Dr. Takamura to schedule the surgery?

KYUSHU (noncommittally)

You can tell him.

(Dr. Frizzel nods, then exits quietly.)

SCENE SIX

The Attendant is isolated in the
hospital.

ATTENDANT (reciting traditional
prayer)

"I may be first, others may be first. It may be today or it may be tomorrow.
Whether one dies later or earlier, death is unceasing, like the falling of dew
on the tip of a leaf. One may be proud of his red cheeks in the morning,
and then turn into white bones in the evening.

(The Nurse enters, rolling in a table of
bright, clean surgical instruments.)

"The wind of change has already come."

(The Attendant reaches inside his shirt,
goes to Kyushu, who also stands
apart.)

I wanted to give you this.

KYUSHU

What is it?

ATTENDANT (removing the bundle)

A furoshiki Sadako's friends left her. I hid it in my shirt, so the doctors
wouldn't steal it...when she died.

(He hands it to her.)

KYUSHU

Why didn't <u>you</u> keep it?

ATTENDANT

I thought you should have it.

(Hinting she should open it.)

What's inside?

KYUSHU (untying the square cloth)

Things...she would have liked.

(The Attendant leans in closer, to see.
Kyushu holds up a pretty hairbrush.)

You could have sold this.

ATTENDANT (nodding)

Probably....But I would have been "muga-muchu!" A man without a <u>self</u>,
without a <u>center,</u> eh?...I'm simply too honest.

(He smiles down at the lovely objects.)

Although an honest man can starve these days.

KYUSHU (taking a packet from the cloth)

Have some rice candies.

ATTENDANT (taking them)

Thanks.

(He moves back away from the bed, as Takamura enters, dressed for surgery.)

I know what's frightening you, Sensai—

TAKAMURA (independently, to Kyushu)

There's nothing to be frightened of.

(He quickly checks the instruments, and the Nurse helps him on with his gloves.)

ATTENDANT

I've heard them too.

KYUSHU (climbing onto the bed)

What've you heard?

ATTENDANT

The ghosts.

(Takamura steps in front of Kyushu, to examine her eyes prior to the surgery.)

We were joking before, you and I. But this time of year, around August the sixth...the memorial of the A-bomb...the ghosts get restless. They walk through the halls, stopping in rooms, looking for. . . .

KYUSHU

What? What do they want?

ATTENDANT

I don't know....I don't know.

TAKAMURA (casually, to Kyushu)
(Kyushu slowly lies back, and the Nurse covers her with a surgical sheet. As Dr. Takamura begins the delicate surgery on her eyes, the Attendant squats down, peasant-fashion, eating the candy, staring ahead, preoccupied with his story.)

Please lie back.

ATTENDANT

You hear them. Walking behind you. Dogging your steps. Hungry ghosts....
> (The actions of Takamura momentarily take the focus. Slight pause. Attendant sucks on another piece of candy.)

The old ones'll tell you to leave food when you expect... ancestral souls to visit. So every August 6th, I go to the memorial, and I take a rice ball...to appease the ghosts. Put them to rest.
> (His tone shifts, becoming defensive.)

I know what you're thinking. "If you don't care about the hibakusha, why do you go to the commemoration of the A-bomb?" Not because of the survivors! Everyone talking about how "We lost so-and-so in our family," and "We lost so-and-so and so-and so in ours!"—Like they're pleased to've been part of this rare experience! But there are also people who died that no one remembers. The "Voiceless voices." And when August 6th comes around... that's who I think of....I can't stay away. I take the rice ball; I say prayers for the people killed; I look at the crowds, and the lanterns in the river.
> (He shrugs, stands.)

And then I go home.
> (Slight pause. Takamura concludes the surgery, places a paternal hand on the girl's shoulder.)

TAKAMURA (sympathetically)

I've done all I can. The rest is up to you. Sleep awhile.
> (Both Dr. Takamura and the Nurse exit. The Attendant follows them, rolling off the metal table. The room is now silent, the feeling there barren and desolate. The light in the hospital has grown dim, streaked in mist and shadow. Footsteps are heard, shuffling into the room. Kyushu sits up. Two Japanese citizens enter, their clothes battle-worn, and not contemporary. They seem exhausted, from carrying a stretcher back and forth. On their stretcher is a body, covered by a dirty cloth. They carry this stretcher to Sadako's empty bed, sit down wearily.)

STRETCHER-BEARER (whispering)

So many dead bodies. What can they do for them?

KYUSHU (whispering to them, harshly)
You can't leave bodies here. It's a hospital.

SECOND BEARER (nodding, to his partner)
It's all they can manage to move them from place to place.
(They stand and transfer the body onto the bed. Then they exit, without acknowledging Kyushu's comment. Pause. She goes to the bed, and stands over it; she cautiously pulls back the cloth. Under it is the Cockroach woman.)

COCKROACH WOMAN
Dozo? Wata kushi-ni...o-mizu-wo? [Please? Give me a drink of water?]
(She sits up weakly. There is a moment of indecision, as Kyushu steps back from the burnt figure, frightened.)
Dozo? Mizu? [Please? Water?]
(Kyushu moves away, averting her eyes.)
Why don't you answer me?...I'm only a person.

KYUSHU
I'm scared. I...don't want to look at you.
(Slight pause.)

COCKROACH WOMAN
How old are you? To be out alone, with this fire and smoke. You're just a girl....I have a girl, two years old. And a strong little boy.
(Kyushu is silent. The woman persists.)
I thought they'd be alright. They weren't...burnt like me. But something happened. And they started crying.

KYUSHU
A lot of children were crying.

COCKROACH WOMAN (confused)
Where are they? Have you seen them?

KYUSHU
No!...I'm sorry. I can't tell you...where they are.
(Pause.)

65

COCKROACH WOMAN

They were trapped in our house. I dug them out. I carried them to safety. But something made them sick. Maybe that rain, after the fires. Black, like oil. It stuck to our skins, made the river look like Chinese ink....Did you see the rain?

KYUSHU

I was hiding under a bridge. But I saw it.

COCKROACH WOMAN

What were you doing?...

(Kyushu doesn't respond.)

Were you lost too? So many people....That's why I must find my children....

(Pause. When the woman resumes her story, Kyushu allows herself to listen.)

We stopped by the river, I remember....They said they were thirsty, but you couldn't drink that water, black as it was, with dead fish floating on it. Then Motoji, my ten year old, complained his stomach was burning—and began to throw up. And the baby began to throw up too....

(She begins to cry, recalling it.)

I went to get help. I called, but no one heard. They were all too busy with their own suffering. No one wanted to hear anyone else. But I kept calling and calling, until I became thirsty too....So very thirsty....

(She stops, staring ahead. Kyushu goes to her bed, to get the glass and pitcher.)

KYUSHU (quietly)

Koko-ni arimasu. [Here it is.]

(She brings them to the woman, fills the glass with water, hands it to her.)

COCKROACH WOMAN

Thank...you.

(She drinks, holding the glass carefully with both hands. Kyushu refills it.)

KYUSHU (quietly)

Your children are dead.

(Slight pause.)

COCKROACH WOMAN (simply)

Are you certain?

66

                    KYUSHU
I saw them. I couldn't tell you.

                    COCKROACH WOMAN
                    (suddenly anxious)
But I have to <u>find</u> them. They'll be frightened.
                    (She struggles to get off the bed.)

                    KYUSHU (touching her, to calm her)
Not anymore. They...were quiet....They looked very peaceful.

                    COCKROACH WOMAN
Where were they?

                    KYUSHU
Outside your house.

                    COCKROACH WOMAN
They weren't crying?

                    KYUSHU
No. They lay there, curled together. Just like they were sleeping.

                    COCKROACH WOMAN
What was it...that happened to us?

                    KYUSHU
A bomb was dropped. To end the war.

                    COCKROACH WOMAN
Did it end?
                    (Kyushu nods.)
Was everyone killed?

                    KYUSHU
Not everyone.

                    COCKROACH WOMAN
Ah. Good. Someone has to remember.
                    (The woman starts to move, painfully.)
I can't stay here, I have to go home. My children will be waiting for me to
come back. I don't want them to feel...they've been forgotten. Arigato, little
girl. Thank you. For helping me.

(She shambles out, leaving Kyushu
alone in the hospital. Slowly, mist and
shadow dissolve, burnt away by the
warmth of the morning sunlight. Behind Kyushu, Dr. Frizzel sits, clipboard
on her lap.)

FRIZZEL

The request for water has special meaning in your culture, doesn't it?

KYUSHU (staring off, after the woman)

I think it does.

(Slight pause. She turns to face
Frizzel.)

Yes. It's supposed to...bring the spirit back to a dying person. To give them
life.

FRIZZEL

But you didn't know that when you were five, did you.

KYUSHU

No.

(Pause.)

FRIZZEL

Did you know her children had died?

KYUSHU

After she'd gone for help, I saw the boy carrying the little girl up from the
river bank. They laid down near the house. After awhile two men came by,
with a large sheet of building tin as a stretcher. They put the children on it
and carried them away. That's when I knew they were dead.

FRIZZEL

And you were under the bridge, watching this?

KYUSHU

Yes.

FRIZZEL

Why didn't you respond, when she called for help?

KYUSHU

I was frightened! She was dead—looked dead....I didn't want to face her.

                          FRIZZEL
Because you wanted to save yourself?

                          KYUSHU
I don't know!...No. I don't remember thinking that.

                          FRIZZEL
I don't think you did either. I think what you did was very normal—hiding —
because you were frightened by her.

                          KYUSHU (facing the morning sunlight)
Shouldn't I have helped her though?

                          FRIZZEL
Would it help if I said that you should or shouldn't have? You feel you
should've done something, don't you? But by not venturing out from under
the bridge—by avoiding the rain and contact with radiation—you probably
saved your life.
                          (Kyushu holds up her hand, studying
                          the light as it comes through her
                          fingers.)
You're alive. You're very lucky.
                          (Kyushu lowers her hand.
                          Takamura has entered, and watches
                          her reaction.)

                          TAKAMURA
Of course you can't expect perfection! But you can see, you have eyes....
You are very fortunate.
                          (He smiles. Steps closer.)
How is the patient this morning?

                          FRIZZEL
I believe she's much better.

                          TAKAMURA
The salutary affects of our hospital food, no doubt.
                          (To Kyushu, who still faces the light.)
How do they feel?

                          KYUSHU
Like a shadow's been removed.

                          (Takamura steps in closer, to examine
                          her eyes.)

                          69

                    TAKAMURA (satisfied with what he
                    sees)
Good. That's an apt description....What do you want to see first?

                    KYUSHU
How much the city's changed.

                    TAKAMURA
I think you'll be amazed at the way it looks to you now.

                    NURSE (entering quietly)
Excuse me. A man in a uniform brought a little girl for the lady doctor. I left
her in your office.

                    FRIZZEL
That would be my daughter. I'd better get her.
                    (She and the Nurse exit.)

                    TAKAMURA (more seriously)
How are you feeling?

                    KYUSHU
Ready to get out.

                    TAKAMURA
I have no doubt. I'd like you to wait, however. So we can watch you a while.

                    KYUSHU
Are you afraid I'll get sick again?

                    (Slight pause.)

                    TAKAMURA (with simple candor)
I can't promise you won't. But then you know that, don't you?
                    (She nods. Pause.)
I've been observing...a number of people lately...who've lost hope entirely
....People who lose the will to go on. And when I see them...with their "thou-
sand mile stare"...I wonder at my own ability to continue....
                    (He shakes his head.)
So many are sick. So many are dying. But I have to keep on, I have to
think ...there's still something we can do to improve things.
                    (He looks at her, hesitates.)
Before you leave, I'd like to discuss what you plan to do...when you "get
out."

KYUSHU (nodding; quietly)

That would be helpful.

(From the back, the Attendant brings in the wheelchair, bearing a Japanese boy.)

ATTENDANT

Doctor? A new patient.

(Takamura excuses himself, goes to the new patient. The Attendant steps over to Kyushu's bed, surreptitiously.)

Good morning, wise guy. You got your sight straight?

KYUSHU (studying him)

I guess not....You look as crooked as ever.

ATTENDANT

Very funny. But you can't upset me today, I feel very good.

KYUSHU

Did you go to the ceremony?

ATTENDANT (very self-satisfied)

Yes I did! I took my rice ball, and I placed it there as an offering, with a sincere sense of reverence. And when I got home, I slept. Very peacefully.

(Sitting on the side of Kyushu's bed.)

But something occurred to me while I was there: No one really wants to remember. All those people, they just want their lives to be ordinary again.

(He lies back, pops a rice candy into his mouth, as Kyushu stands, watching him.)

These days...when there's so much that we have...when we can buy TVs and radios, electrical appliances...why should we waste our time thinking about the bomb? I don't mean anything profound! I'm just saying...we have to get on with life. Consider that, Sensai.

KYUSHU

Don't call me that. You're just making fun of me.

ATTENDANT (standing up)

No, no, not at all, you teach me many things!

(Whispering:)

If I wanted to make fun, I'd call you "tenno heiko" [His majesty the Emperor] —and I'd salute you!

71

(He does so comically, then
concludes:)

But if it bothers you, I'll call you something else...."Ryoshinteki"—because everyone needs a conscience.

(He starts to go, then stops.)

It's as they say: "A man can get direction...from a child he carries on his back."

(He smiles, laughs, and exits. Dr. Frizzel returns, with a girl in American clothes.)

FRIZZEL

Kyushu, I'd like to introduce you to my daughter. Lilly, this is Kyushu. She's a patient here. Would you like to talk with her, while I meet someone?

LILLY

Sure.

(Her mother strokes her hair, then goes to see the new patient. Slight pause.)

I was in a hospital once. They took out my tonsils. Is that like what you're here for?

KYUSHU (indicating Dr. Takamura)

You'd have to ask him. I've never had tonsils taken out.

LILLY

It hurts. But you get over it.

(Slight pause.)

My mom said you don't have parents.

KYUSHU

That's right.

LILLY

I live with my grandparents. In America. Have you ever been there?

KYUSHU

No. Hiroshima's the only place I've been.

LILLY

Do you like it here?

KYUSHU

I haven't.

72

LILLY

Why didn't you leave?

KYUSHU

Well,...I thought if I was going to die,...this was a good place to do it.
(She smiles. Lilly looks confused.)
I'll need a better reason now.

LILLY

A lot of people died here, huh?

KYUSHU

Yeah.

LILLY

We went to the Memorial Day—at the park with the statues about the bomb.
And people were floating paper lanterns on the river, with candles burning
inside. There were thousands of them! And they twinkled like stars. Mom
said that each one was for someone who'd died in the bomb....

KYUSHU (hesitates, then explains
simply)
Each lantern has a name written on it. They drift down the rivers, out to the
sea, where they burn—as you said—like thousands of stars.
(Slight pause.)

LILLY

Do you hate me, Kyushu?

KYUSHU

No, I don't hate you. Why would I?

LILLY

Because of the war. Japanese kids call me names and things—things I
don't even understand. And it's just because I'm American, I think.

KYUSHU

A lot of people are still angry. But not just at America. At war itself. For
what it's done.
(Lilly hasn't understood it all, but she
has listened. Kyushu reaches under
her bed, takes out a lantern and other
materials.)
I've been making this, from things a friend left me. Would you like to see it?

73

LILLY

Sure.

KYUSHU (letting Lilly hold it)

Maybe you can help me with it.

(She places a small candle inside it,
and then ties a string to it, to suspend
it.)

LILLY (looking at it)

It's very pretty. But there's no name on it.

KYUSHU (as lights slowly isolate
them)

No. I've drawn these pictures instead. Here's a crane, flying over the city.
And below it, a mother—carrying her children to safety.

LILLY

It's very pretty.

KYUSHU (pointing to a spot in front)

Let's hang it there.

(Lilly climbs off the bed, ties the lantern
to the end of a bamboo pole that one
of the children has carried on in the
dark area surrounding the bed.
Kyushu lights a long match, hands it to
Lilly.)

You can light the candle.

(Lilly lights the candle inside the lantern. She sits down beside Kyushu on
the bed. Kyushu places an arm around
the girl's shoulder, as they look up at
the lovely flickering light in the lantern.
The Lights Fade, until only the lantern
is visible.)